THEN AND THERE SERIES
CREATED BY MARJORIE REE
GENERAL EDITOR: JOHN FINE

The Home Fro... in the Second World War

PAUL FINCHAM

Illustrated from contemporary sources

LONGMAN GROUP UK LIMITED,
Longman House, Burnt Mill, Harlow,
Essex CM20 2JE, England
and Associated Companies throughout the world.

Published in the United States of America by Longman Inc., New York.

First published 1988

Set in 11/13 point Rockwell Light (Linotron)
Produced by Longman Group (F.E.) Limited
Printed in Hong Kong

ISBN 0 582 22360 1

Acknowledgements

We are grateful to the following for permission to reproduce photographs: BBC Hulton Picture Library, pages 7, 45, 59; Imperial War Museum, pages 15, 22, 25, 29, 30, 34, 39, 43, 48, 57; Popperfoto, pages 17, 19; *Punch*, page 53; Topham, page 9; Mrs Wreford, Felixstowe, page 11.
Cover: War Weapons Week in a Country Town by Michael Ford, 1941. Photo: Imperial War Museum.

Contents

To the reader

I was almost eight when the Second World War started. My friends and I knew that something bad was happening, but we didn't really understand what war meant. Tunnels were dug on our school field and seats put into them. Men came to school and gave each of us a black rubber gas mask: we wore these for five minutes every day. Other men came to paste netting over the windows and we couldn't see out. Often, a horrible noise filled the air: it was the air-raid siren, said our teacher, practising, to get us used to it. We called the noise 'Moaning Minnie', which made it seem less alarming.

When the 'phoney war' ended and things really started to happen, we walked one day to see the first bombed house in my town. We looked at the roof hanging off, the furniture and clothes blown into the garden. Could an aeroplane fly over and drop something that could do this? We had the uncomfortable feeling that the next bomb might fall on *our* house.

Then the Battle of Britain began and parents wondered about evacuating their children. I was sent only a little distance, into the country, which seemed safer. I didn't like the village school, or the other children, and they didn't like me. I was glad to come home at Christmas 1940. For the rest of the war, my school days were like those of most other children. We raised money for the Red Cross, collected salvage, gaped at bomb craters, and forgot all about fireworks, Christmas crackers, bananas, or lemons on pancake day, which just weren't there any more. School went on as usual, but we were always 'making do', even over staff. One year, my class had three different mathematics teachers in three terms. Almost everyone using this book will have friends or relatives who lived through the war. Talking to such people is probably the best way of learning about the Home Front. One word of warning: remember that people sometimes invent details, if their memories are not so good as they think.

Words printed in **thick black** are explained in the Glossary on page 64.

1 The 'phoney war'

The war begins

When the air raid **sirens** wailed dismally, on Sunday morning, 3 September 1939, Britain began six years of war. Nobody knew then how long it would last. That first siren was a false alarm but nobody knew that either. For more than a year, most people had thought there would be war with Germany. Now that it had come, they expected bombs and gas attacks at once. Many were not sure what they should do when the warning sounded. One boy remembered his father rushing round the house, closing windows. A mother, out with her children, thought of pushing them into a ditch and covering them with grass.

Older people remembered air raids twenty years before, in the First World War, and everyone expected that, if war came, enemy planes would be overhead immediately, bringing death and destruction. In fact, the war began quietly and people were soon joking that it would be over by Christmas. Hitler, the German leader, they said, had made a mistake in thinking that he could frighten the British.

The government tried to prepare for war, making everyone realise that they must expect to do certain things, or go and work in certain places, whether they liked it or not. If your country needed you to fight as a soldier, or do special work, you could not refuse unless you had a good reason. To give the government power to make people obey orders, Parliament passed many **emergency laws**. Local councils were ordered to arrange Air Raid Precautions (ARP), to organise first aid, ambulance drivers, fire-watchers, and all the work of **civil defence**. More than a million people volunteered for these jobs. They formed groups and set up headquarters in schools or church halls, learning and practising what to do when attacks came. Some produced their own newspapers and magazines, with ARP rhymes, to help them learn:

In a raid, don't lose your head,
Just remember the things you've read.

Taking cover

Every household received a booklet called *The protection of your home against air raids*, and shops, offices and private houses all began making some kind of shelter. Householders used the space under the stairs. Towns built big underground public shelters for the people of whole districts. Schools dug similar ones in their playgrounds, for teachers to shepherd the children into when the siren sounded. Senior boy pupils sometimes helped with digging, half frightened and half excited at the thought of bombs dropping from the sky. People filled sacks with sand and stacked them round doors and windows, to provide cover from bomb blast. They glued net or tape over windows. Then, if the windows shattered, the tape held the glass in place, preventing deadly splinters from flying in all directions.

Poor families were given an Anderson air raid shelter, and better-off people could buy one. It was made of curved sheets of corrugated steel, bolted together, and buried four feet deep, with earth on top. If you fitted your Anderson out carefully (like a caravan) it held six people. (Some of these shelters still sit dumpily in back gardens, used as apple or coal stores.) They were usually cold and damp, and people preferred the indoor shelter – the Morrison – issued in 1941. This was a steel table with mesh sides, and you crawled underneath. Children liked the Morrison: its top was useful for games, or model railway layouts, and if you had to get inside, you could pretend to be a wild animal in a cage.

Anderson shelters were named after Sir John Anderson who, as Home Secretary, was responsible for Air Raid Precautions. If they were covered with 15 inches (37 cm) of earth, they were strong enough to resist everything except a direct hit from a bomb. These shelters are being delivered to a London street even before war began.

Evacuation

In spite of the shelters, the government thought it was best to get people away from towns where bombs would probably drop. They offered schoolchildren, and mothers with babies, the chance to be evacuated – sent to a safer place – usually in the country. In four days the railways carried more than a million **evacuees** in nearly 4,000 special trains. The children took spare clothes and food for the journey.

Each child had a postcard to send home and a label with his or her name and address. Many had never been away and did not want to leave their mothers. One six-year-old girl was heard telling off a younger weeping one: 'You'll cry the writing off your label and they won't know who you are.'

Many of the children went in school groups, with teachers in charge. Some groups, especially those from boarding schools, had prepared for evacuation, hiring large houses or arranging to share another school's buildings. But most simply went to the big London railway stations without much idea where they would be sent, and there were all sorts of muddles. Trains left when full, so some schools got split up. Some who had arranged a place to go found themselves going in the opposite direction.

When coaches and trains arrived in villages or towns in a 'safe' area, there were more muddles when people came to collect the children they would give homes to. The cleanest and brightest looking were grabbed quickly, so the men and women whose job was to find homes for everyone had to trail round, persuading someone to take the left-overs. Farm families snatched up strong looking boys, who might be useful. Later, teachers spent days tracking down all the children from one group.

One large party arrived at an east coast seaside town where schools had to be opened as make-do homes. Children and grown-ups slept on sacks of straw and lived on milk, cheese and apples until homes were found. Yet at other places there were not enough evacuees to go round, and people who had prepared a welcome went away disappointed.

The air raids and bombing did not happen, and people

Opposite: Evacuee children arriving at their new home, with a policeman helping the teacher to unload his pupils. Notice their luggage: the little suitcases and paper bags; the square cardboard boxes containing gas masks; and the labels, with the children's names and addresses. From their faces, how do you think that this group felt about being evacuated?

CKL

were soon laughing about this 'phoney war', which was not a war at all. Evacuees missed the town life, with shops and cinemas. They did not like the countryside. 'Where's the chip shop?' was the first question many had asked. By the new year, 1940, two out of every three had returned to their homes in the cities.

Gas masks

Because the Germans used poison gas against our soldiers in the First World War, we expected them to use it against civilians in this war. Everyone got a gas mask (respirator), with orders to carry it always. Children who got to school without their masks were sent home to collect them. I never got used to wearing mine and knew I couldn't keep it on for long. Small children, who might be scared of the ordinary kind, had special red and blue masks, with large ears. They were meant to look like Mickey Mouse. Not everyone found them funny. One helper remembered how 'they all howled' when he tried to fit them on. Mothers could put babies into gas 'helmets' and pump air in for them, but while this was happening the baby sometimes turned scarlet!

Animals

Some people evacuated their pets, like their children, to safer areas, but thousands had them destroyed. The RSPCA estimated that 400,000 dogs and cats were killed in the first week of war. Some owners of small zoos had their animals destroyed too, in case bombs blew open the cages, letting the animals escape. In fact, camels at one zoo did not even bother to stand up when a bomb fell near them, although a colony of monkeys ran wild for days after the wall of their home was broken. London Zoo drained the huge aquarium, in case both fish and water were released in a bomb blast. It also destroyed its poisonous spiders and snakes. Food for pets was a problem throughout the war. Some birds and animals enjoyed carrots, but it was hard

A class of infants with their teachers, practising gas mask drill and seeming to enjoy it. The sandbags on the right are piled up around the entrance to the air raid shelter, to give more protection against bomb blast.

to get fish for penguins and sea lions. A visit to any zoo in wartime was disappointing, with so many cages empty, and only a label to explain which animals had been there.

The blackout

If you didn't want the enemy to bomb you, you tried not to be seen from the air. Buildings were painted green or brown to blend with the landscape. A boy cycling through Sussex in 1940 noticed how an airfield's buildings were **camouflaged** and the hangar roofs draped with gigantic leaf covered nets. However, it was impossible to disguise something like Canterbury cathedral, or huge greenhouses. Motorists sometimes painted their cars in dull colours. Others thought that the best way to camouflage a car was to let it get really dirty.

At night the problem was different. People needed light, but had to screen it so that aeroplanes saw a town as a smudge of light, not a brilliant glare. Air raid wardens, checking the blackout, took their duties seriously. One warden prosecuted a man who lit a match in the street to find his false teeth which had fallen out. At dusk, windows had to be blacked out with thick curtains, or with a frame covered with black paper, which clipped over the window like today's double glazing. One family who did this found, on waking grannie next morning, a hole punched through the paper screen over her window. 'All my life I've watched dawn breaking,' she snapped, 'and I'm not stopping now.'

A clergyman's wife found that her rectory had more than fifty windows. Big factories, hospitals, and buildings with oddly shaped windows, had the hardest work. Sometimes people painted over the glass and kept the lights on all day. Churches held evening services in the afternoons. Schools gave up concerts, clubs and all events which would need blacked out windows. Later, they came round to arranging some sort of curtains or shutters, if only for a few rooms.

The sudden and complete darkness in the streets caused many accidents. Nearly twice as many people were killed on the roads between September and December 1939 as in the same period of 1938. Gradually, rules were made a little easier, with car headlights screened, not totally switched off. Pedestrians were told to wear something white or luminous so they showed up in the dark. Anyone showing lights after dark was prosecuted. A farmer grumbled that nobody could shut seventy cows up for the night without letting a flicker of light escape. And strange encounters happened all through the war. A woman bumped into something very large she could not recognise. It was the elephant from a local circus, returning home for the night.

Being evacuated to a strange part of England; spending the night with neighbours in a shelter; travelling on business in blacked out trains and buses; colliding with strange objects in dark streets: such unthought of things suddenly became part of everyday life. One good thing was that people very soon became friendlier and more helpful to each other than they had been before war broke out.

Things to do

1. If you live in a town, imagine how you would feel at being evacuated to the country, living in a strange house, going to a different school, and missing all the familiar things at home. If you live in the country, imagine a bunch of 'town' children coming to share your home and school. Write a story about this, called 'Evacuees'.
2. Make a chart, with pictures and notes to explain them, about the preparations for war. It should include evacuation, gas masks and the blackout, but you should be able to think of others.
3. Discuss whether you think the preparations for war were sensible. Remember we now know a lot of things that weren't known then.

2 From the 'phoney war' to the Battle of Britain

The Germans invade Europe

In April 1940, Prime Minister Neville Chamberlain joked about the war. 'Hitler has missed the bus,' he said. A few days later, on 9 April, Germany invaded and occupied Norway and Denmark. A month later, on 10 May, Hitler turned on the Low Countries: Holland and Belgium. His aeroplanes bombed towns, his soldiers and tanks poured through the countryside. Holland, then Belgium, quickly surrendered and the Germans began to swarm across France.

In May 1940, Winston Churchill replaced Chamberlain as Prime Minister. Although he promised only 'blood, toil, tears and sweat', his determination to beat the Germans gave Parliament and people more confidence. They certainly needed it. In France, our army, the British Expeditionary Force (BEF), which had been sent there when war began, was driven back towards the coast at Dunkirk. The government decided on a rescue attempt. On the radio one evening this announcement was heard: 'The Admiralty have made an order requiring all owners of self-propelled pleasure craft between 30 and 100 feet in length to send further particulars of them.' The harbour at Dunkirk was destroyed, so the plan was to collect men from the shore in these small boats and ferry them to larger ships further out at sea.

The Dunkirk evacuation

'Operation Dynamo', the evacuation code name, began on 26 May and ended on 4 June when the Germans were too near for more men to be rescued. 338,000 men were lifted

Soldiers, photographed at Paddock Wood railway station in Kent, on 1 June 1940, after their rescue from Dunkirk. The Medical Corps officer is handing bundles of socks into a train compartment. The boxes under the arm of his lady helper suggest that she begged her batch of socks from the local men's clothing shop.

from the sand hills, where they huddled, hiding from German planes screaming overhead.

At the south coast ports where they landed, extra trains were brought from all over England. Seriously injured men went straight to hospital. Ladies of the Women's Voluntary Service (WVS) washed blistered feet and mended socks. At one station, fifty women worked for a week, making sandwiches. Others handed out blank postcards for the survivors to let their families know they were safe. The soldiers were so tired that they fell asleep immediately, and people still remember seeing trains trundling through country stations packed with silent sleeping men.

Winston Churchill warned against too much rejoicing: 'Wars are not won by evacuations.' Things still looked bad for Britain. Italy, under the leadership of Mussolini, joined the war on Germany's side on 10 June, and later that month France surrendered, leaving Britain on its own. Hitler expected Britain to ask for peace. When this did not happen, he made it clear that he was prepared to invade Britain, just like the Low Countries and France.

The Home Guard

The government decided to form a special voluntary force, not part of the regular army, to defend Britain. Anthony Eden, Secretary of State for War, appealed by radio for 'large numbers of men. . . between the ages of seventeen and sixty-five.' The name of the new force was the Local Defence Volunteers (LDV) but it was soon changed to the Home Guard. Men and boys raced each other to the local police stations to enlist: a quarter of a million in the first twenty-four hours. By the autumn there were one and a half million, many of them youngsters not old enough for the forces. The men met and trained anywhere they could: church halls, scout huts, barns. Their only uniform was an armband with the letters LDV. Some carried homemade weapons: sticks, hammers or chair legs. Before rifles were issued, one officer sent his men out with bags of pepper to throw in the invaders' eyes. Later on, the Home Guard became more soldier-like. There were weapon training sessions when the men got rifles and they learnt how to throw **grenades**. They also learnt how to fight in the streets and how to prepare homemade fire bombs to hurl at advancing tanks.

By autumn the Home Guard were being issued with uniforms and carrying out a good deal of work previously done by the army. They guarded railway bridges, reservoirs and telephone exchanges which an invading enemy would need to control or destroy. They built road blocks. They stopped cars and checked who the occupants were,

A soldier, with his LDV armband, checks a driver's identity at a road block. The name LDV was changed to Home Guard on 23 July 1940. Because of blackout regulations, one of the car's headlamps has no bulb and the other is masked, to show only a faint light. Sometimes, after many of these stops and checks, drivers lost their tempers and were arrested.

from the **identity cards** that everyone carried. A few motorists who objected to all this, accusing the Home Guard of 'playing at soldiers', were actually shot after refusing to stop at a road-check.

Preparing for invasion

Those summer months after Dunkirk, when we expected a German invasion, were anxious ones. Once again, children from London, East Anglia and the south-east were sent away from the danger zone. The government wanted to clear dangerous parts of the coast. They took over sea front premises and filled them with army or Home Guard units. Boats, which might help an enemy, were removed. So were beach huts. Huge concrete blocks were put on the beaches, making it harder for trucks and tanks to land. Coils of barbed wire stood where deck chairs and sand-castles had been. People left seaside towns. Clacton went from 25,000 down to 4,000; Folkestone from 46,000 to 6,000. German guns in France could bombard towns across the Channel, and the records of one church include entries like 'Evensong, shelling during service'.

The poster 'Careless Talk Costs Lives' reminded everyone not to give away information. People became suspicious of strangers. Along coasts, senior schoolboys, in-between examinations, patrolled the shores and cliffs in case enemy agents landed. One boy remembers having an ancient machine gun but no bullets. He decided that, if necessary, he would simply throw it at the enemy. To confuse parachutists if they dropped, place names were removed: that is, signposts, the names of village shops, church notice boards and names of railway stations. Police and Home Guard were given some 'test' words to use on suspicious persons, who might say them the wrong way. They included 'clothes', 'wretch', 'tough' and 'through'.

Fields, parks and open spaces where aircraft could land were littered with old cars or farm machinery, to stop them. A young cousin and I, convinced that we were being helpful, threaded empty tins on ropes and strung them across the garden each night, to trip up the paratroops and clatter a warning to the neighbours.

The Battle of Britain

The Battle of Britain was fought in the skies. It began with a series of daylight raids on 10 July 1940, and went on through August and September. It was Hitler's attempt to destroy the Royal Air Force (RAF) and gain control of the air, for his plan 'Operation Sea lion' – the invasion of England. 1940 was an exceptionally fine summer. Day after day the blue skies over south-east England were filled with aeroplanes and criss-crossed with white vapour trails as the RAF's Spitfires and Hurricanes, and the **Luftwaffe's**

Through the summer and autumn of 1940, although the Battle of Britain was being fought above south-east England, farm work had to go on as normally as possible. People working in the fields dashed for cover only when it was necessary. These children of hop pickers in Kent are crouching in a ditch at the side of a field but still keeping their eyes on the sky, watching – and probably enjoying – the dogfight going on up there.

Heinkels, Junkers and Dorniers, engaged each other in **dog-fights**. The wreckage of crashed aircraft lay in the fields all around and people collected pieces for souvenirs.

Newspapers published the figures as for a cricket match: 'Biggest raid ever: score 78–26, England still batting'. After the war we found that these figures were exaggerated. Three pilots might claim to shoot down the same plane. When the RAF claimed 182, on the fiercest day, 15 August, the real total was 75. The RAF pilots, some only a year or two out of school, often landed after one mission only to find that there were no reserves and had to take off again with no rest time. 'We were too tired even to get drunk,' one of them remembers. Winston Churchill, in praising their bravery, told Parliament: 'Never in the field of human conflict was so much owed by so many to so few.'

Things to do

1. 'Careless Talk Costs Lives'. Explain what this meant and write a short story to show how it might have happened.
2. If you had been rescued from Dunkirk, how would you have filled in the blank postcard to send to your family, letting them know you were safe and describing your arrival back in England?
3. People still talk about the 'Dunkirk spirit'. What do you think they mean?
4. Draw a map of south-east England, the Channel and the French coast. Mark Dunkirk, and the ports where the survivors were brought back to England.

3 The blitz

The beginning

Near Croydon, in Surrey, a boy bicycled up a hill one brilliant Saturday afternoon. From the top he had a grandstand view of a colossal air attack. It was 7 September 1940 and the **blitz** was just beginning. For the next eight months, London had hardly a single peaceful night. By the end of the year, nearly 14,000 Londoners and 10,000 people elsewhere had died in air raids.

That Saturday afternoon, the bombers' first target was the London docks. The bombs started great fires, and when the planes returned after dark, they were guided by the blazing warehouses. Firemen at Woolwich Arsenal fought the fires among crates of live ammunition and highly explosive nitroglycerine. Warehouses full of rubber, sugar and paint sent flames and sparks high into the sky like some fantastic firework display. In one store, a pepper fire filled the air with stinging smoke. In another, wheat turned to a sticky mess which pulled the firemen's boots off.

The bombs rained down on the little streets of tightly packed houses behind the docks, the homes of thousands of workers and their families, in Stepney, Poplar, Millwall, West Ham and other places. They were poorly built and whole streets collapsed in dust and rubble. People searched for relatives among the ruins. A few 'rest centres' were set up, usually in schools. One doctor remembers how **refugees** poured in, their hair and skin ingrained with dirt, so that hosepipes were needed to get them clean. Later, these centres became better organised but in these early days there were few beds or blankets and little provision for meals. One centre, at Bethnal Green, had only one knife and two spoons.

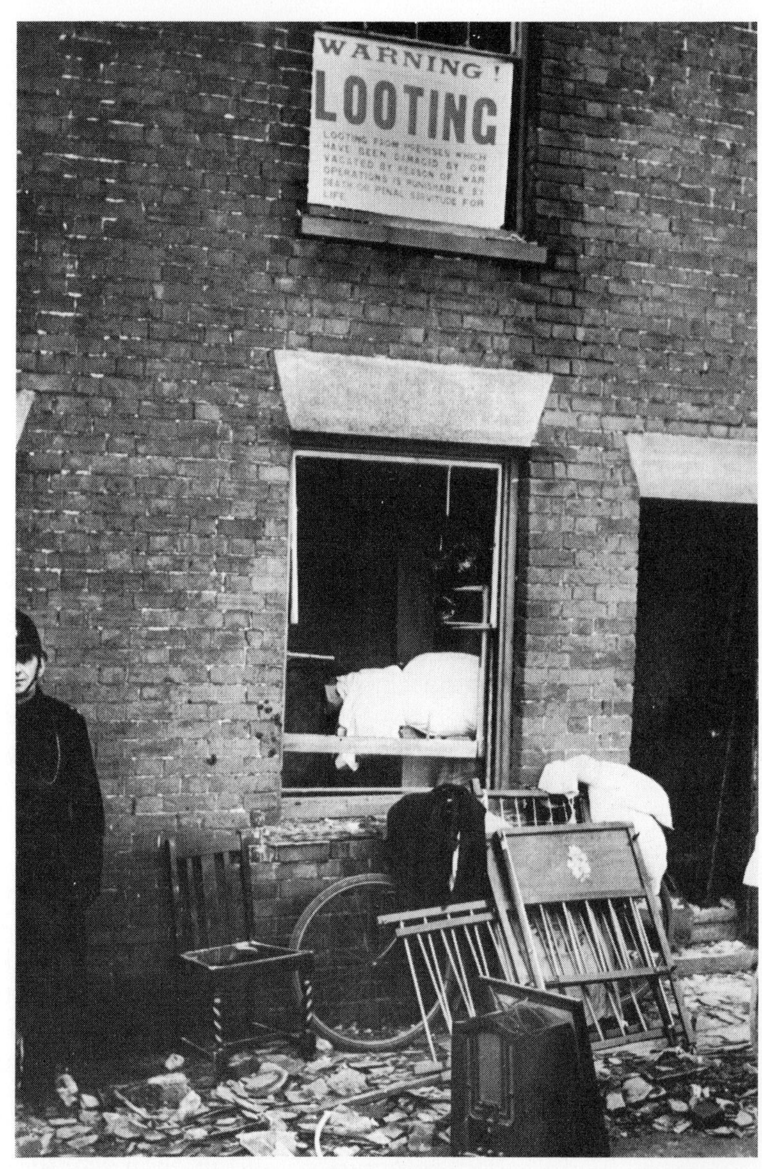

A policeman guards the wreckage of bombed houses in south-east England in March 1943. Furniture and belongings which might still be of use – beds, chair and radio – have been brought outside. The notice warns people not to steal from bomb-damaged buildings: 'Looting from premises which have been damaged by or vacated by reason of war operations is punishable by death or penal servitude for life.'

To escape the bombs, thousands of people left London (and other cities when they too were bombed). Epping Forest to the north-east, Hampstead Heath and Greenwich Park all seemed safer than the built-up areas. But many never took shelter, like the old lady who said: 'It's not worth going – nowhere's safe.' Of those who did, a great many went every night into the underground railway stations. They began queuing in the morning (the doors opened mid-afternoon), and soon all space on the platforms and in the passages was 'bagged' by piles of bedding. One person (often a child) could reserve places for the whole family, whose members arrived later, after work. They brought picnics and thermos flasks, played cards, or exchanged 'bomb' stories. When the trains stopped and the electric current was cut off, the shelterers spread out. Some slept on the escalators or even between the rails. At dawn people began leaving, perhaps to get an hour or two in bed before the day began. For some whose houses had been destroyed the 'tubes' became home. They seemed safer than they were. That autumn and winter several stations were bombed and people died in them, sometimes from blast, sometimes drowned when water pipes burst.

Through September and October the raids spread to all of London. That boy who saw the blitz begin recorded in his diary that Regent Street, the Strand and Trafalgar Square had been badly damaged, as well as suburbs like Clapham and Wimbledon. But he also noted: 'London is so huge that at least half isn't touched.' People even managed to joke about their problems. A shop whose windows were blown out had a sign saying 'More open than usual'.

The blitz spreads to other cities

As winter approached, the Luftwaffe began making raids on other big industrial cities, where factories produced all kinds of munitions. The first was Coventry. On the night of 14 November, more than 400 planes dropped high explosive and **incendiary bombs** there, killing more than 500 people. Nearly one-third of Coventry's houses were not fit to live in. Two hospitals and twenty factories were hit and the cathedral was burnt out. Telephone, gas, water and electricity supplies were wrecked. Soldiers moved in to help, and the WVS brought **mobile canteens** and cooked meals in the streets, for helpers and survivors to have some hot food. Yet in ten days Coventry pulled itself together and its factories were in full production again. By then, the bombers had moved on: Birmingham, Southampton, Liverpool, Hull, Clydebank, Portsmouth and Plymouth all suffered. In Bristol, where the king and queen went to see the damage, the king asked one woman where her house was. 'You're standing on it, sir,' she replied. The king set up the George Cross and George Medal to reward civilians for extreme courage. One medal went to a telephonist who stayed at her switchboard, even when her clothes and hair were smouldering.

The bombs

Most bombs were the high explosive kind but there were variations. One was the delayed action bomb, or UXB. By the end of October 1940, 3,000 of these were waiting to be defused and each meant that the surrounding district must be cleared until the bomb went off or was made harmless. One, buried under St Paul's Cathedral, took the Royal Engineers three days to remove.

Land mines were really sea mines, dropped silently by parachute. Sometimes these too were booby-trapped not to **detonate** at once. A family heard a crash at the back of their house. They couldn't open the kitchen door so went out of the front door and peered through the back windows to see what was jamming it. A cylindrical mine, eight feet tall, had plunged through the roof and lay propped against the door!

Strange bombs, each like a tin can with two sprouting 'wings', were often found in the streets. From their shape they were called butterfly bombs. If you picked one up, it could explode, killing or injuring you. After one air raid on Grimsby in 1943, these butterfly bombs caused many

IN AN AIR RAID . . .

HOW TO FIGHT A FIRE

Have your equipment ready and tell someone to look out for fire.

This shows a stirrup hand pump in action.

If you cannot put out the fire *quickly*—call the Fire Brigade or Auxiliary Fire Service. Make sure you know the quickest way to do so.

CLEAR AWAY INFLAMMABLE LUMBER FROM ATTICS AND TOP-FLOORS, IN ADVANCE

Government posters, with helpful advice, were displayed everywhere. People laughed about them, but they were a good way of reminding you, through pictures, of what to do or how to act when there was danger. This one explains how to deal with a fire started by incendiary bombs. Why is the last sentence an especially useful piece of advice?

casualties when people came from the shelters and picked up the curious objects.

Incendiary bombs caused the most trouble. Aeroplanes dropped them in clusters, 'like fireflies coming down', thought one woman. As they fell, they gathered enough force to drive them through a roof, where they burned, setting the roof alight. A two hour incendiary attack on London, just after Christmas 1940, started 1,500 fires, most of them in the City where they fell into unattended office blocks and burned unchecked. After this, fire-watching became compulsory for men aged sixteen to sixty and, later, for women between the ages of twenty and forty-five. Organisers worked out rotas so that your turn came round once a week. The government encouraged householders to keep buckets of sand or water ready, and a scoop, to remove incendiaries. They supplied some **stirrup pumps** but people often bought their own. By 1943 there was at least one in every street, with a small notice on a gate – 'stirrup pump here' – showing where it was. The basements of bombed buildings sometimes became great water tanks, to ensure enough water to deal with incendiary fires.

Fire-watching duty was unpopular but it certainly helped save property in later raids. In 1942 the Germans bombed the historic towns of Canterbury, Exeter, Bath, York and Norwich. When 6,000 incendiary bombs fell on Canterbury, it was the fire-watchers' prompt warning that saved the cathedral from the same fate as Coventry's.

Things to do

1. Write a short story about how people occupied themselves during long nights spent in the London underground during the blitz.
2. Draw a map of England and mark on it all the towns mentioned in this chapter as being blitzed.
3. Hitler expected the blitz would make Britain give in. Why didn't this plan work?

4 Helping the war effort: 'make do and mend'

When war began, shops were well stocked. As they sold out, replacements were difficult or impossible to get. There were no spare ships to import foreign goods, and at home almost everything was turned over to war production. Factories which once made buttons, or zip fasteners, now made cartridges. So people looked for ways of 'making do', repairing things they would once have thrown away and trying to use something else in place of what they really needed. Even those who had collected a store of useful things found their stocks used up as the years passed. Hairgrips and combs, soaps and cosmetics, were never seen in shops. At a wartime village sale, I was disappointed to win some elastic in a lucky dip, but found I was popular with all the ladies, trying to buy my prize from me!

In every street, posters encouraged you: 'Save Waste Paper', or 'Dig for Victory', or 'Buy Defence Bonds'. Magazines had hints from readers on how to make do. One found beetroot juice a good substitute for lipstick. When stockings were unobtainable, some girls coloured their legs. One recommended a sand and water mixture, painted on. Another, with a sense of humour, told how children yelled 'old Oxo legs' after her, when she dyed her legs with gravy browning.

Clothes

When the government introduced clothes rationing in 1941, they kept their plans secret, to stop people panicking.

Everyone had sixty-six coupons (later reduced to forty) each year. You needed sixteen coupons for a coat, eleven for a dress. At the same time, **austerity** regulations were made, to save materials. Skirts must not have lots of pleats and only short trousers could be made for boys. These regulations did save material but were unpopular. People tried making clothes from unrationed things. Blackout material, embroidered, could become a skirt; sugar or flour sacks (if you could get them) could be dyed and made into curtains. And if you could find someone who did not need all their coupons, you might be able to buy them, although this was against the law. The WVS organised sensible exchange meetings where people could change clothes they no longer needed. Schools, where children quickly outgrew things like football boots, found it useful to do this too. Jumble sales attracted long queues well before they opened.

Women and war work

By 1943, only a woman with very heavy family responsibilities could avoid doing some sort of war work. Most were sent to munitions factories to work long hours at unpleasant tasks. It was all part of the 'war effort'. Factory bosses, scornful of the women at first, were amazed at the results. Some nervous girls never got used to hard work. Others who had been housewives or had had dull jobs like shop assistants, enjoyed the new wartime experience and the chance of earning money. In one town, women were doing the repairs to coal barges. One said: 'Well, we get mucky, but the work is lovely.' Some professions, like teaching and nursing, had refused to employ married women before the war. Now they welcomed them. By the time war ended, women were accepted in all jobs once thought suitable for men only: crane drivers, welders, blacksmiths, house painters, and others. There were always more jobs than people to do them.

National savings

The war was costing Britain £13 million a day by 1944. Half came from taxation, and the government borrowed the rest from the people, who were earning more than ever before, in the form of national savings. More than 300,000 savings groups were started, in streets, schools, factories, even air raid shelters. Housewives ran many of these groups, finding time each week to call at every house for the money. Schools did their collecting along with the other routine jobs, and wall charts showed the latest totals. Each year there was a special savings week. In 1941 it was called War Weapons week; in 1942, Warships week; in 1943, Wings for Victory week; and in 1944, Salute the Soldier week. Every town and village had its celebrations.

Children at Blean village school, in Kent, advertising War Weapons Week (1941), when the village target was £450. The graph shows how much money has been raised so far. The government hoped that if people *saved* their money as national savings, they would have less to *spend*, and this would stop prices rising too much. An unpleasant cartoon character appeared on posters, to persuade people not to be tempted into extravagant spending. 'Don't help the Squander Bug' was the message. Notice the school windows criss-crossed with tape (see chapter 1).

There might be a dance, a comic football match against an army team, perhaps a parade of the local Home Guard – all to persuade people to save more and more. Towns set targets, agreeing to raise certain sums but really hoping for much more. In one village, Salute the Soldier week had a life-size figure of a soldier guarding a pile of money bags. The pile grew as the week went on.

Salvage

> There'll always be a dustbin,
> To save for Victory,
> So treat it right, and let it fight
> For home and liberty.

The government urged people not to waste anything. Tins, rubber, rags, bones and paper could help the war effort.

Containers for them stood at street corners. Sometimes there were **salvage** drives when special efforts were made. Children always enjoyed helping and trundled carts round, collecting. In 1943, when paper was scarce, there was a Book Drive. Fifty-six million old books were collected in a few months. Some went to the forces and some to libraries which had been bombed, but most were pulped for paper. Some sharp eyed people spotted and rescued rare books which turned up this way but many more must have been destroyed.

Early in the war, housewives were asked to give up their aluminium for scrap metal to make aeroplanes. Many handed over saucepans and kitchen utensils. Later, the government ordered the removal of iron railings round parks, gardens, even church yards. More than a million tons were sawn off and carted away. Most of this metal still lay, piled in great heaps at the collecting dumps, when the war ended.

Things to do

1. Imagine yourself a newspaper reporter, writing about Wings for Victory week in 1943 in your nearest town. If you can look at the newspaper files in your town library for the first half of 1943, you should be able to find some details about what happened. (Your teacher will explain how to set about this.) Another way to find out is to ask older relatives if they remember these savings weeks and use their memories in your report.
2. Design a salvage poster (the photograph on page 30 will help you) asking people not to waste anything and illustrating how salvage helps the war effort.

Opposite: Salvage exhibitions, like this one at Oxford, were regularly organised, to remind people how useful scrap metal, rags and paper all were to the war effort. The display here shows how the metal from a crashed aeroplane could all be re-used. School visits to these exhibitions encouraged pupils to collect salvage even more keenly.

5 Feeding the people

Food rationing

People shopping on 8 January 1940 had to take something new with them – their family's **ration books**. At first, only bacon, ham, butter and sugar were rationed. Meat followed in March, tea in July, jam, marmalade, cheese and margarine the next year. Sweets were not rationed until July 1942. Long before then, they were seldom seen in shops but – like many other things – were kept 'under the counter' for favourite or regular customers.

The Minister of Food, Lord Woolton, rationed food so that what was available was shared fairly and everyone got enough to keep them fit. Many people were healthier during the war than ever before because they were having to eat things which were good for them. In newspapers and on cinema screens, Dr Carrot and Potato Pete encouraged people not to waste food.

Those who have the will to win,
Eat potatoes in their skin,
Knowing that the sight of peelings
Deeply hurts Lord Woolton's feelings.

Digging for victory

The government urged people to 'dig for victory'. Flowerbeds became cabbage patches, lawns were dug up for peas and beans, and even roadside verges were made to grow something. Groups of neighbours formed pig, goat, rabbit and poultry clubs, to get extra milk, or eggs, or meat. There were occasional problems: a family might find it could not face eating a bird it had fattened up for Christmas dinner.

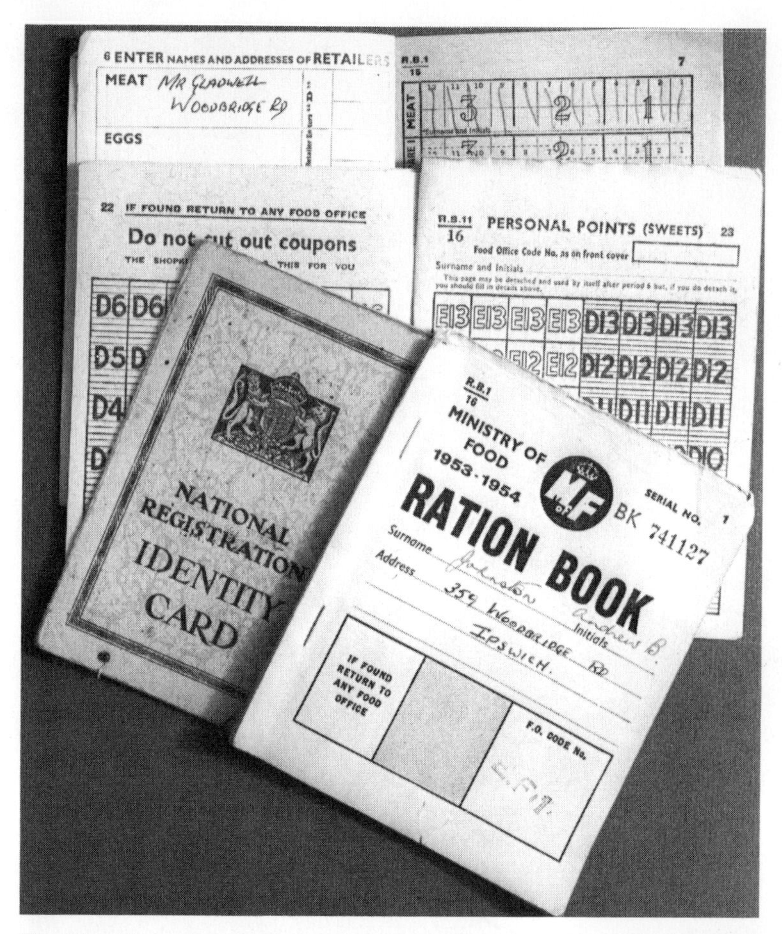

The identity card, issued to everyone, had the owner's name, address and National Registration number. My number was TVNN. 117.6 because I was the sixth member of my family. My father's number was TVNN. 117.1. The ration book had coupons for different foods, which the shopkeeper cut out when you used them up in buying something. Some foods were still rationed, as you see from the date on this book, in 1954, nine years after the war ended.

Farmers were paid to plough up grassland and wasteland, and by 1942, six million extra acres had been cultivated. Most of this reclaimed land grew carrots, potatoes or sugar beet. Farm workers were not called up because their work was so important, and the Women's Land Army

At Bethnal Green, in London's badly bombed east end, these boys helped the war effort, and supplemented their families' rations at the same time, by making vegetable plots on a bomb site. With a lot of digging, forking and raking, they gradually turned the devastated back yards and tiny gardens into a space where some kind of crops could be grown. The wrecked houses stand in the background.

(WLA) was recruited to help them. These 'land girls' worked hard for long hours, doing jobs they had hardly heard of before the war. Two in Lincolnshire became famous as rat catchers, trapping 12,000 rats in one year.

Some schools ploughed up their playing fields and gardening replaced games on the timetable. As the war went on, schoolchildren often helped on farms, for example with the potato harvest. In 1943, 70,000 boys helped like this. Farmers who for years had considered children on farms a nuisance now praised their hard work.

Shortages and substitutes

Many children grew up in the war with no idea what tropical fruits were like. Occasionally a soldier abroad would bring some home. One soldier once brought me two coconuts. One I ate (with help from the family). The other coconut I was made to raffle, raising £1 (a lot of money in 1942) for Red Cross funds. Later in the war, when British soldiers were in Italy, they sometimes sent home almonds or lemons. The arrival of such a parcel caused tremendous excitement. Favoured friends would be given half a lemon or a handful of nuts, the first they had seen of these items for years.

Because so many foods were scarce or unobtainable, all sorts of substitutes were tried. People used dried elderberries as currants in cakes and puddings. Parsnips, flavoured with banana essence, made a good banana spread for sandwiches. Sweets were made from condensed milk and cocoa, and a horrible lumpy ice-cream from custard powder. With food so precious, any sort of waste was a tragedy. One family, starting supper when bombs began falling, dived under the table, and came out again to find their dog eating the lot. A mother left her baby in the pram while she was shopping. She came back to find that the baby had sprinkled a packet of tea all over the road. It was the ration for two people which was supposed to last for a whole week.

People queued for a long time to get any kind of unrationed food. After standing an hour and a half on a bitter February morning, one woman got three herrings. Another waited an hour for a few slices of tongue. People were reluctant to leave a food queue even when the siren sounded. 'It was worth it,' said one woman. 'I got half a pound of liver.' A girl staying in the country in 1940 wrote to her friend that the local boys had been shooting blackbirds. 'They all eat them in the village here,' she said, and added that sparrows were also good, but you needed such a lot of them for a pie.

Canteens

To make their rations last longer, everybody tried to have some meals away from home. Before the war, only a quarter of a million children had dinner at school. When it ended, two million were having school dinners, and twice as many were having free or cheap milk. The number of factory canteens increased twelve times. More than 2,000 'British Restaurants' were set up in towns. They served food like stew and vegetables, followed by treacle pudding and custard. The government's 'Food Facts' booklet had another rhyme to encourage people to eat there:

> Where are you going to, my pretty maid?
> To our British Restaurant sir, she said.
> May I come with you? That would be nice,
> They have very good meals at a very low price.

Because the factory canteens and British Restaurants were often run by first-class chefs from luxury hotels, the meals they served were some of the best available in wartime. But these chefs despaired of their customers who, they complained, usually only wanted fish and chips and cream cakes, wouldn't eat salads, and refused any sauce unless it was brown and came from a bottle!

Things to do

1. Design a 'food in wartime' chart to show: food you couldn't get, food which was rationed, some of the substitutes which were used.
2. Find out why the wartime diet was considered to be a healthier one than that eaten before or after the war.

6 Being at school in wartime

One morning after an air raid, two little boys going to school were chattering about the night's events. 'Perhaps the school windows are broken,' said one. 'Let's hope so,' replied the other. In lots of ways, the war was exciting rather than frightening for children. They rather enjoyed the interruptions that worried and upset adults.

Changes in routine and staff

Any school which had no air raid shelter in September 1939 had to stay closed until one was made. Senior boys helped to dig shelters on the playing fields. Then some schools in 'safe' areas found evacuated schools sharing their buildings. Village halls were borrowed as extra classrooms, or one school might have lessons in the mornings, the other in the afternoons. Classes joined together, and fifty or sixty children squeezed into one room.

More than 20,000 male teachers joined the forces. Before the war, women teachers who married had to give up their jobs. Now they were asked to return and some retired teachers were persuaded to come back until the war ended. Many found themselves teaching subjects they knew little about. In my school, the French master taught biology lessons, textbook in hand, keeping just one page ahead of us. Most classrooms had a big world map with little flags showing where the fighting was, so geography lessons suddenly became more real. Sometimes a school 'adopted' a ship, or an aeroplane. The children wrote letters to the crew, sent them books and magazines, and were occasionally rewarded by a visit from some of the men on leave.

Air raids at school

If a night air raid lasted more than two hours, school began late next day. If it lasted more than six hours, school was cancelled. But there were daytime raids when pupils had to take cover. These were welcomed if they interrupted an unpopular lesson. We huddled on benches in the draughty shelter, hoping that the all clear would not sound until the maths lesson ended

For the staff, the worst difficulties were air raids during important summer examinations. In 1944, when flying bombs (V1s) constantly arrived over southern England with no warning except the sound of their engines, supervising teachers told examination candidates to fall flat on their faces between the rows of desks. (It was a good chance to hiss 'What's the answer to question 5?' at a friend.) One school sent an explanation away with its examination papers: 'Ten minutes extra time allowed because so much time lost getting under desks.'

Shortages

In the war-time school, nothing was wasted. Books were repaired long after they were worn out because there were no new ones. Pupils wrote in the covers of exercise books and ruled extra lines on each page. Paper was of such poor quality that scraps of straw could be seen in it. If the pen stuck in one, ink spattered over the page. Needlework classes were given over to patching, knitting socks for the army, or making soft toys from scraps. Food was too precious to let schoolgirls practise cookery. Instead they learned about nutrition and healthy foods, like oatmeal and lentils. It was hoped that they would pass this on to their mothers.

Sports equipment got more and more dilapidated, and games suffered in other ways. One Kent school lost its cricket pitch when a bomb fell. At another, boys cleared bomb splinters and empty shell cases from the field before playing games.

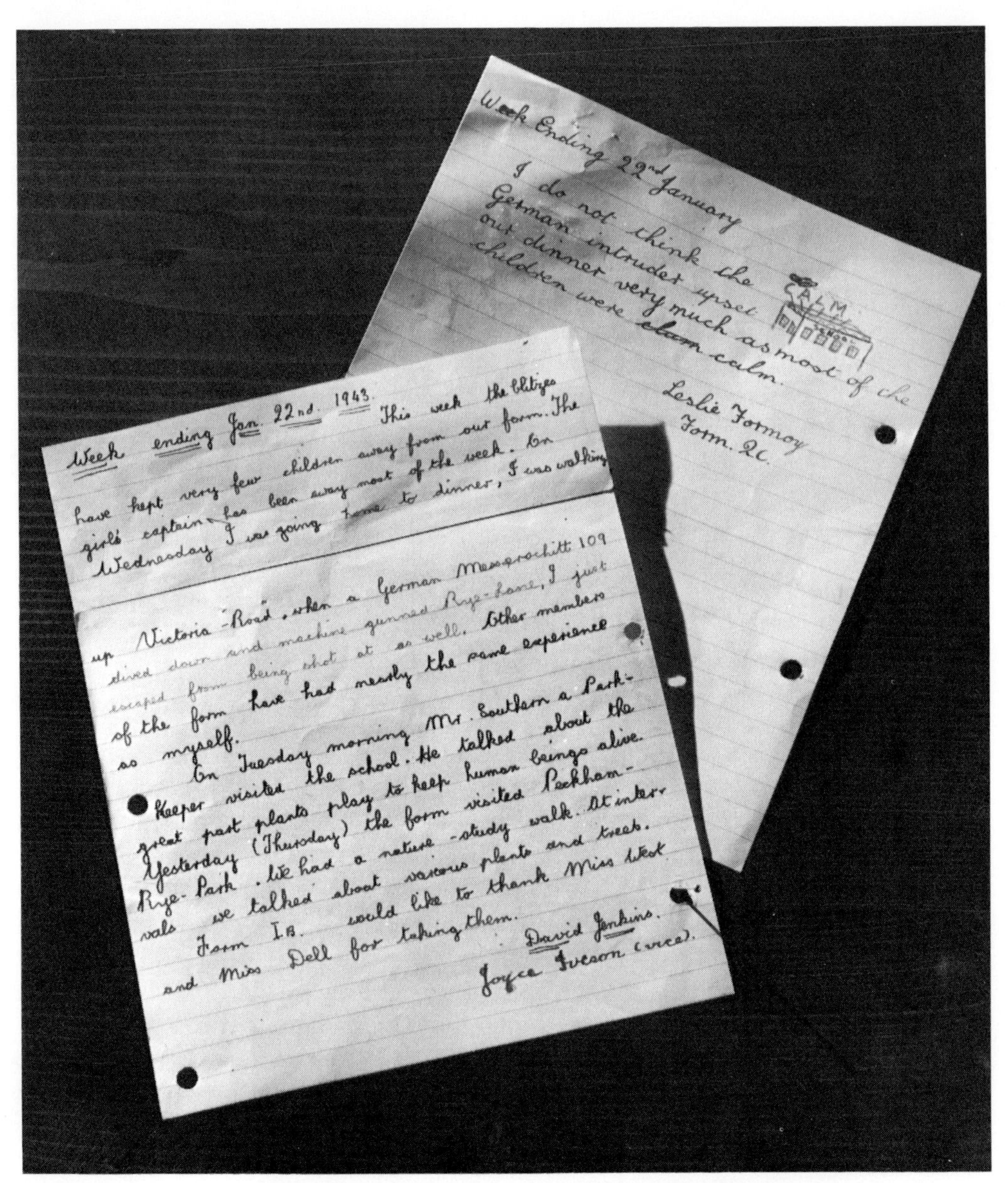

Week Ending 22nd January

I do not think the German intruder upset our dinner very much as most of the children were ~~clam~~ calm.

Leslie Formoy
Form. 2C.

Week ending Jan. 22nd. 1943. This week the blitzes have kept very few children away from our form. The girls' captain has been away most of the week. On Wednesday I was going home to dinner, I was walking up Victoria-Road, when a German Messerschitt 109 dived down and machine gunned Rye-Lane, I just escaped from being shot at as well. Other members of the form have had nearly the same experience as myself.

On Tuesday morning Mr. Southern a Park-Keeper visited the school. He talked about the great part plants play to keep human beings alive. Yesterday (Thursday) the form visited Peckham-Rye-Park. We had a nature-study walk. At interval we talked about various plants and treats. Form IB. would like to thank Miss West and Miss Dell for taking them.

David Jenkins.
Joyce Iveson (vice).

Two pages from a class diary, for January 1943, show how calmly these children reacted to being machine-gunned by a stray German aeroplane. The park-keeper's visit, and the nature walk, may have been part of the campaign to encourage schools to collect medicinal plants.

Games and hobbies

All sorts of war hobbies flourished. Small children played Spitfires versus Messerschmitts in the playground, shooting each other down with machine gun noises. Older boys formed spotters' clubs. A small book on sale showed the outlines of all British and German planes, and children learnt to model them in balsa wood. Another hobby was collecting shrapnel, fragments of bombs and shells. A Cambridgeshire village once had a short, sharp raid of incendiary bombs. They were quickly dealt with, then the schoolchildren went out and collected more than 200 tail fins, which they brought back to school for an exhibition. Similar displays, with a small admission charge, were often held for Red Cross funds. When flying bombs began arriving, there was tremendous competition to collect pieces. One boy who rescued a whole tail fin hid it in a sack in case the authorities confiscated it.

School children and the war effort

At a time when everyone was helping the war effort, teachers encouraged children to do the same. Hobby clubs went in for practical subjects, like gardening, rabbit keeping or shoe repairing. Homemade toys found a ready sale at Christmas time. Older children could spend several weeks at harvest or forestry camps, working and enjoying themselves at the same time, making up for not having seaside holidays. Senior schools, with help from local factories, sometimes used their workshops and laboratories to make simple parts for tanks or planes. There was always some kind of salvage drive going on, and schools were ideal bases for the scrap metal or paper or whatever it was, to be brought and sorted. A newspaper reported that Devon children collected 4,000 pounds of bones in their summer holiday.

Country schools made collections of a different kind. Their boys and girls gathered herbs and wild flowers to replace medicinal plants not being imported. Clover heads, coltsfoot leaves, foxglove seeds, poppy petals and dandelion roots were all useful. Seniors collected the poisonous plants: belladonna, henbane and thorn apple. Juniors gathered rose hips to make syrup. They kept sacks in school and sent them to factories when they were full. The money they got went to the school funds.

Things to do

1. Write a letter, as if you were living at this time, to a friend in a part of England not much affected by the war. Describe how your own school life has changed and tell about some of the odd things that might happen in an average day. Re-read the extracts from the diary on page 39 before starting this.
2. Between 1939 and 1941, juvenile crime in England and Wales increased. Small thefts increased by 20 per cent and malicious damage by 70 per cent. Why do you think this was? (It may help if you discuss this with your teacher.) Make up a diagram to show these figures and illustrate some of the things that make children behave wrongly.
3. If your school existed during the war, it may still have its log book, a kind of day to day diary which the head teacher keeps. You might get some interesting, or surprising, information if you are allowed to look at the wartime entries.

7 Getting about in wartime

Is your journey really necessary? asked the posters at railway stations, bus stops and street corners. The question was supposed to make you feel guilty about travelling, using space and fuel that ought to be helping the war effort. Certainly nobody travelled for fun. Wartime journeys were expensive, uncomfortable, and sometimes even dangerous.

Cyclists and pedestrians

Cyclists found it almost impossible to get new bicycles, tyres, pumps, or lamp batteries. Pedestrians, using 'Shanks' Pony', found the blackout dangerous. They bumped into all sorts of things at night: pillar boxes, lamp-posts, sandbags and other people. Country walkers could fall into ditches or find cattle straying across their paths. So black was the blackout that people could get completely lost, especially if going from a brightly lit room straight into the darkness.

The war saw the beginning of what we call hitch hiking, begging a ride from someone in a vehicle. A young man working in London but living in the suburbs did this regularly. He enjoyed being 'hauled aboard' a van by a crowd of workmen or finding himself one evening in a smart sports car.

Motorists

Petrol rationing began on 22 September 1939. The day before, people flocked to garages to fill cans and bottles with it. Motorists had an allowance based on their car's

Bus and train journeys were so difficult and unpleasant that people were only too glad to use 'Shanks' pony', which meant their own legs. Before the war, only one family in every ten had owned a motor car, so people did not miss driving everywhere as much as we would, fifty years later.

size which let them travel about 150 miles (240 km) per month. The ration was reduced several times, and in 1942, when every drop of fuel was needed for the forces, there was none for ordinary citizens. Britain had two million cars in 1939. By 1943 there were only 700,000 on the road, mostly belonging to people like doctors or farmers with special needs. Even they had to have a government permit for spare parts. Many people laid up their cars 'for the duration', draining radiators and petrol tanks. After the war, no new cars were made for some years and lots of these old ones were coaxed back to life for a time.

Bus travel

Bus services had their fuel supplies cut too and had to economise. Few buses ran after 9.30 p.m., and usually none on Sunday mornings. (A popular song of the time was 'We mustn't miss the last bus home'.) More and more people squeezed into those buses that ran. Seats were often re-arranged, facing inwards, to let more people stand. Sometimes a bus was so heavily loaded it could not climb a hill unless passengers got out and walked. Everyone had to queue, and the London Passenger Transport Board invented a character, 'Billy Brown of London Town', to set a good example. One of their rhymes said:

He never jostles in a queue,
But waits and takes his turn. Do you?

Bus services ran during air raids unless bombing made it impossible. Bus drivers had nasty shocks in the blackout: they sometimes drove into a bomb crater or pile of rubble. Unexploded bombs forced drivers to find another route. One bus wanting to cross the Thames had to try five bridges before finding one that was not ablaze or closed because of UXBs (unexploded bombs). Bus depots were often bombed. At one, twenty-nine buses were burnt out when their petrol tanks exploded. Coventry lost half its buses in the blitz. Some towns borrowed buses from each other. In 1940, buses came to London from as far away as Exeter and Inverness, returning home with labels saying 'London 1940–41'.

Rail travel

A passenger from London to York in 1942 found the train so crowded that he spent the whole journey 'on the concertina part connecting two coaches'. Wartime trains were slow, dirty and always crowded. Carriages, corridors, guards' vans and even the lavatories were all packed, mostly with servicemen, whose bulky kitbags, gas masks and rifles took up most of the room. At night things were worse. With closed windows, drawn blinds and almost no lighting, compartments got hot and stuffy. One woman remembered how a party of munitions workers from a Midlands factory, on finding a train already packed, just broke up all the tables and threw them out, to make more standing room.

Passenger trains were often delayed to let war supplies

Besides destroying gas and water mains, and electricity and telephone cables, bomb craters were a great danger for vehicles. This one, at Balham in south London, was deep enough to hold a London Transport bus which drove into it. The photograph was taken in October 1940 at the height of the blitz. During that autumn and winter, 156 London Transport workers were killed and 406 were injured.

pass. People watched for what seemed hours as trucks carrying guns, tanks or aeroplanes rolled past them. At one time, 1,700 freight trains moved rubble from bombed cities to build airfield runways in the south and east. Spring 1944 brought more interruptions when tens of thousands of troops moved south, ready to invade Normandy on 6 June.

Trains, like buses, continued running during air raids, with drivers often under great strain. Sometimes ammunition trains had to be moved from blazing sheds, or goods trains shunted past unexploded bombs. Engineering staff dealt promptly with bomb damage, filling craters, shoring up tunnels and rebuilding bridges. (104 railway bridges were out of action for a time during three weeks of the 1940 London blitz.) Stations tried to keep travellers informed of timetable changes, by loudspeakers and notices, but they were sometimes put out of action themselves. In the blitz, all the big London stations were damaged at some time. Once, at Waterloo, books and papers from the newspaper kiosk were blown everywhere, and the ticket machines were blasted the length of the platform.

Things to do

1. Draw a block diagram to compare the number of cars in Britain in 1939 and 1943. Ask in the library for post-war figures to add to your diagram.
2. Ask older relatives if they 'laid up' their cars during the war, and if so, how and where they did it.
3. Describe a wartime bus or train journey as though it happened to you. You could do this in the form of a letter written to someone after the journey, letting them know what it had been like.
4. You can find out what happened to your local bus company in the war by looking it up in the index of your local newspaper. (If there is an index, it will be in your local public library.)

8 Wartime holidays and Christmases

Holidays

Holiday makers abroad in August 1939 hurried home when they realised war was coming. As they crossed the Channel and saw guns on the white cliffs of Dover, they must have guessed that there would be no more holidays overseas for a time. Next year, as the holiday season began, Germany invaded Holland, Belgium and France. The government cancelled the Whitsun holiday, and the south and east coasts soon bristled with barbed wire and tank traps. Royal Engineers laid mines on beaches and blew up piers to stop the enemy landing. Some big holiday camps and hotels housed troops or foreigners who had been arrested.

Although a few places like the Lake District or the Derbyshire Dales remained peaceful, travel was so difficult that most people could not make long journeys. For the rest of the war, the government persuaded them to take 'stay-at-home holidays'. Local councils arranged entertainments in parks, with band concerts, Punch and Judy shows, swimming galas, sports tournaments and beauty contests. With few cars on the roads, people enjoyed country walks and picnics, although one family abandoned theirs quickly when a stray German plane bombed the field where they were relaxing. Greyhound and horse-racing, and football matches, were always popular. The famous players were all called up, and teams sometimes borrowed a few spectators in order to have a game at all.

At dances, girls found plenty of partners among the troops stationed locally. Some dance halls admitted soldiers at half price; other lent them shoes, to save their floors from damage by army boots. Long queues formed outside cinemas, even in bad weather. Newsreel films were especially popular. Good humoured audiences cheered when Mr Churchill appeared on the screen, and booed Hitler and Mussolini.

Christmas

The first wartime Christmas was not a hard one. Food was not yet rationed and shops still had stocks of presents. Many toys and games on sale had a 'war' flavour: toy helmets and rifles, soldier or nurse uniforms, and model kits of ships, planes and tanks. Jigsaw puzzles carried pictures

These children, using one London air raid shelter during the blitz, invented their own entertainment. They made glove puppets, improvised a stage and curtains with some help from adults, and produced their own Christmas puppet show.

of land and sea battles, and one 'Happy Families' card game had groups of fighters and bombers instead of the usual characters. New board games appeared, called 'Invasion' and 'Blockade'. Presents for grown-ups had a wartime look too. One favourite was a fancy gas mask container.

By Christmas 1940, things had changed. London and other cities were blitzed, and nearly everything was scarce. A lorry arriving at one market with cases of oranges and lemons caused such chaos that the police were called. Magazines had recipes for 'wartime Christmas pudding' or '**economy** mincemeat'. A girl noted in her diary that, before making their pudding, her family had waited a month for a hen to lay an egg, 'and yesterday she did it!' The emphasis this year was on useful presents. Sleeping bags or thermos flasks for the air raid shelter, and torches for the blackout, were among the suggestions. Christmas cards were smaller, and printed on flimsy paper. Wrapping paper and labels were harder to find.

The BBC's special programme, 'Christmas under Fire', told of air raid shelters where paper chains hung from the bare walls and the wardens wore party hats. One shelter in the basement of a West Ham church celebrated Christmas cheerfully, in spite of gunfire overhead. Carol singers came in, Santa Claus brought toys and clothes, and the shelterers enjoyed a traditional Christmas dinner, and a party afterwards.

There were four more wartime Christmases, and each got drearier. After 1942, new toys virtually disappeared from the shops. Second-hand toys and games were eagerly bought up: thirty people applied to buy a china doll within an hour of it being advertised, and the first one secured it. People made soft toys and wooden toys. A little girl longed for a dolls' house. Her parents, despairing at first, made a beauty from an old birdcage. The WVS organised toy exchanges, for children to change their old familiar toys with other children.

It was harder to find substitutes for Christmas food. Mothers brought precious tins of pineapple or peaches from their dwindling pre-war store cupboards, and covered plain cakes with 'mock' marzipan made of almond-flavoured crumbs. Magazines suggested dipping holly in Epsom Salts to make it sparkle, for decorating cakes, or living rooms. They also recommended homemade presents. A necklace 'from odd lengths of brightly coloured wool' was a typical idea. A man spending Christmas with friends gave them each a tablet of soap. In return, one gave him an egg, the other an ounce of butter.

Pantomimes were a favourite way of raising money for war funds. Princess Margaret and Princess Elizabeth (now the queen) wrote and acted their own at Windsor Castle. One air raid shelter group acted the story of Cinderella, losing her gas mask instead of her slipper. Hitler appeared as the wicked fairy!

Things to do

1. Ask older people what they most remember about Christmas in wartime, especially if they were at school then. Use what you find out to write a story or design a chart, comparing Christmas in the Second World War with Christmas now.
2. Draw up an imaginary programme for a 'stay-at-home holidays' week in your town or village.
3. What would you miss most if you had to live under war restrictions today?

9 Wartime weddings

Preparations

Planning a wedding, which could take months in peace-time, was done much more simply and quickly now. A woman's magazine reminded every reader that, if the bridegroom was in the forces, she would have to do many of the things that were usually his responsibility, like getting the marriage licence. There was no petrol to bring guests long distances, and rationing made it impossible to hold large receptions, so only a few people could come. The bride's parents, who usually paid for everything, may not have been sorry about this.

Presents

Wartime wedding presents were a problem. By 1941, all the things usually given were either rationed and on coupons, or else unobtainable, so people gave as presents things they already had in store. Sheets, towels, china and glass, cutlery and kitchen utensils were all very accept-able. Nobody minded second-hand presents. One girl, married in 1943, had a 'weird and wonderful' collection, including dozens of glasses 'of all shapes and sizes', and ten tablecloths. Another remembered that her best present was a pound of tea from friends who did not drink tea them-selves, and saved their ration to give to her.

Clothes

Wartime brides usually could not have a traditional white dress unless they could borrow one. Girls preferred to save their clothing coupons for something more useful, so the wedding dress was one that would do afterwards for 'best'. For one wedding, arranged hurriedly because the (sailor) bridegroom had unexpected leave, the girl bought her dress, hat and shoes on her way to church, and put them on in the shop where she bought them. If the groom was in the forces, he wore his uniform, and his bride might wear his regimental badge on her dress. She might also cover the ugly cardboard box holding her gas mask with some kind of pretty material, to carry, along with her bouquet.

Photographs

With photographic materials scarce, the only wedding pictures were often taken by a friend lucky enough to have a film for his camera. A few photographic studios kept going during the war but they were only allowed to take one or two shots of a wedding. Some kept whole sets of brides' and bridesmaids' dresses, to hire out to couples whose wedding they were booked to photograph. If you looked at the pictures displayed in their studio windows, you recognised the same dresses, over and over again, on different brides and bridesmaids!

The reception

The wedding reception was perhaps the hardest thing to organise. With food rationed, hotels and restaurants could not provide elaborate meals, so buffet parties were more usual, and most people thought they were nicer. The Ministry of Food allowed extra rations for up to forty guests. For that number, the caterer could claim ten ounces of butter, five ounces of sugar and two pints of milk. Some people preferred to hold a reception at home. One family made sandwiches from scrambled dried eggs. Another sent all the family members out, that morning, to queue at shops for cakes, getting as many different ones as possible. The wedding cake was a real problem because, after July 1940, bakers were not allowed to make or sell iced cakes. A plain sponge, with imitation cream, was one solution. And at a wedding in my family, the cake was covered in 'mock' almond paste and decorated with chocolate icing, made from cocoa.

"Are you ready to cut the cake, Madam?"

Above: A cartoon from *Punch*, 10 January 1945. Bakers' shops had always kept cardboard models of elaborate wedding cakes, with imitation icing made of plaster, to use for display in their windows. In wartime, one of these dummy cakes, placed over the real one, allowed the bride at least to pretend for a time that she really was having the grand wedding she had always dreamed of.

After the wedding

There was no honeymooning abroad, of course. A weekend in London, or a few days with relatives in another part of the country, was as much as most couples managed. Then it was back to the army, or factory, or whatever the war work was. Most newly-married couples did not have their own house. If the husband was in the forces, the wife probably continued living at home with her parents. If husband and wife were both working, they might be able to rent two rooms in someone else's house. Those who married after January 1941 could claim furniture coupons, or 'dockets': six for a table, five for a bed, and so on. Even so, the shop might have no furniture to sell, even with dockets, so there were often long delays. Young couples tried to buy odds and ends of second-hand furniture at high prices and they dyed old sheets and bedspreads to make curtains. One couple solved some of their problems by collecting bits and pieces from bomb sites and using them to make what they needed. A broken lawn sprinkler became a lamp. Curtain hooks and cup hooks, never seen in shops, were all gradually unearthed by some patient and well planned digging.

Things to do

1. Try to borrow some wartime wedding photographs from relatives, to arrange a small exhibition. Ask them what they remember about the wedding presents and the reception, and write something about these to include in your exhibition.

10 The V weapons and the end of the war

The V1s

A land girl, working on a Kent farm, got up early on 13 June 1944. As she walked to work, and heard a clackety-clacking noise overhead, she looked up and saw 'a black shape, with sheets of flame spurting out behind.' It was the first V1, or flying bomb, to reach England.

British **intelligence** had known for some years about Germany's two 'revenge weapons', the V1 and V2. Mr Churchill tried to prepare the public for 'new forms of attack', and added: 'Britain can take it.'

That first V1 crashed near Gravesend. Another reached London and exploded on a railway bridge. After a couple of days of excited rumours, the government told people the truth about the flying bombs. The doodlebug, or buzz bomb, as it was nicknamed, was about seven metres long, with enough fuel to fly 150 miles. When the noisy engine stopped, it plunged to earth and exploded. Blast did most of the damage, hurling people against walls and showering them with broken glass.

Soon, flying bombs began arriving in large numbers. One, in a shopping area on Saturday afternoon, killed twenty-four people. Wandsworth had three in thirty minutes. A Sunday morning arrival destroyed the Guards Chapel at Wellington Barracks during morning service, killing or injuring over 200. People heard the noise overhead and, if it stopped, flung themselves flat. After the explosion, they got up and carried on. A boy in the cinema slid down in his seat, hands over ears. Another remembered the referee at football matches telling players that three whistle blasts meant lie down. Someone invented a slogan: 'When doodles dive, don't dawdle'.

More people left London. Paddington station one day was 'a solid mass of people'. Those who stayed found good protection in their Anderson or Morrison shelters. Most V1s fell short of London, landing to the south: Croydon, Lewisham and Wandsworth each had more than a hundred. The south-eastern counties of Essex, Kent, Sussex and Surrey were called 'Doodlebug Alley'. More than 3,000 fell there.

V2s

When southern England was getting used to the V1s, a new horror arrived. A school caretaker at Chiswick, crossing the playing field one evening, 8 September 1944, was flung several yards by a blast like a thunderclap. Those first on the scene eyed the enormous crater and thought a gas main had exploded. The government kept quiet about the new secret weapon until mid-November. Then Mr Churchill told the House of Commons: 'For the last few weeks the enemy has been using . . . the long-range rocket.'

The V1 gave you a few seconds to dive for cover. The V2 rocket gave none. One fell while I was in school one afternoon. One minute, the lesson was proceeding normally. The next, there was a bang which shook every door and window and sent everyone running into the corridors. It seemed as though whatever it was must have fallen on the playing field. In fact, it was a mile away, and we went – a few days later – to gaze at the vast hole in a ploughed field.

At 5,000 miles an hour, the rocket could smash through anything. A survivor from one that hit a big shop, killing more than a hundred people, thought it must be an earthquake. Both V1s and V2s did great harm to property as well as life, at the worst period damaging 20,000 houses each day. People often mended windows and repaired roofs just as another landed, and everything needed doing again.

Thirty-five V2 rockets fell on the London borough of Ilford, including this one in March 1945. It killed nine people and injured thirty-four. Eight houses were blown to nothing. Sixteen more had to be demolished, and thirty-three were unfit to live in, while 116 others were badly damaged. You can see in this photograph what a huge area has been flattened. Tarpaulins have been pulled over the roofs of the houses on the left, so that people could continue living there while waiting for the repair gang.

The end of the war

But the war was nearly over for Germany. The **allied** armies who invaded Normandy on D-Day (6 June 1944) had pushed into Europe, capturing the bases which launched the flying bombs and rockets. The last V2 fell in Kent on

27 March 1945. Two days later, a doodlebug, wobbling towards the East Anglian coast, was shot down into the sea. There were no more attacks on Britain, and by the first week of May, Germany was beaten.

Everyone sensed that the war was over but official news was slow in coming. Not until Monday, 7 May, did people know for certain what was happening. At school, we were called together that afternoon: we must listen to the news on the radio, said the headmaster, to find out if the next two days were a holiday. We did, and they were. After 2,094 days, Germany was defeated. It was VE Day – Victory in Europe. It was not quite the end of the Second World War. Japan had also fought along with Germany and the Japanese were still fighting. But the war in Europe had affected Britain the most, and that at least was over.

Naturally the grandest celebrations were in London. The bright lights and fireworks frightened small children, who had never seen either before. Mr Churchill's car was pushed to Westminster when, with tears rolling down his cheeks, he went to tell Parliament: 'In all our long history we have never seen a greater day than this.' Ordinary people had their own thoughts about it. One man felt how good it was to enter a shop or pub without getting tangled up in the blackout door curtain. Another found it hard to imagine life without air raids.

In other towns, too, there was rejoicing. Bands in Derby played outside, for dancing in the streets. People hung out flags and held street parties. Mothers somehow found cakes and jellies, and there were party hats and conjurors and fancy dress parades. One little boy, covered in old clothing coupons, represented 'rationing'. Other people made costumes from old blackout curtains which were not needed any more.

We were still at war with Japan until August, when the new Prime Minister, Mr Attlee, announced: 'The last of our enemies is laid low.' There were two more days of 'VJ' celebrations, then Britain got down to the business of being at peace instead of war.

Parties like this one in London were held everywhere to celebrate VE Day, often in a street closed to traffic for a few hours. The children had not seen so much food in several years. At a Colchester party one small boy ate thirteen jam tarts. Everyone joined in, lending benches and tables, gramophones and records. The party sometimes ended with dancing, and a bonfire, and perhaps somebody would produce a few fireworks which they had hidden away throughout the war years.

Post-war Britain

A few people, over-excited, burned their ration books and petrol coupons, and used up what remained in their store cupboards, but nobody really expected everything to return to normal immediately. The post-war years were in some ways harder than the six years of war, as Britain struggled to get back on her feet. Fuel was often scarce; clothes were rationed until 1949; and some foods were still rationed in 1954. Bombs had killed 60,000 people and injured more than 200,000. Many families had lost relatives, homes and possessions.

For some people, the greatest thing they lost when the war ended was a wonderful feeling of being needed. The war had brought everyone closer together as nothing else could. Now, they missed their work as air raid wardens, ambulance drivers, first-aid workers or fire-fighters. For all its terrible results, the Second World War had made them feel useful and wanted. 'Now there's nothing to look forward to,' was what many of them felt.

Things to do

1. 'When Doodles Dive, Don't Dawdle.' Design a poster with this slogan, and a picture of a flying bomb coming down.
2. Can you think why people hated the V1s more than the V2s?
3. Try to find out, by asking people and looking at the local newspapers for May 1945, how VE day was celebrated in the place where you live.

How do we know?

There are more books and pictures about the Second World War than any other event in history. Some of these books are listed on page 62. Libraries keep files of old newspapers, and those from the war years tell what was happening. Local newspapers reported local news: bomb damage or blackout problems. They published information about events such as the savings weeks (chapter 4) and stay-at-home holidays (chapter 8). The advertisements tell about wartime shortages and prices (chapters 4 and 5). The librarians will know what items of this kind the library keeps.

Cinemas and television often show war films: *Dunkirk* and *The Battle of Britain* are two examples. While such films are useful for their realistic details, we should remember that they may exaggerate to make an exciting story. Documentaries about wartime are safer: they usually include actual newsreel film, shot at the time.

Two London museums recapture the feeling of the war. The London Museum has reconstructions of air raid shelters and many smaller personal reminders. The galleries of the Imperial War Museum are filled with objects, models, and frequent special displays. Its library has photograph albums, and diaries and notebooks kept during the war. Each of these is another piece of evidence, for 1939–1945. On a former Battle of Britain airfield at Duxford, near Cambridge, the Imperial War Museum keeps its collection of aircraft. Spitfires and Hurricanes stand by their German opponents, and a sinister flying bomb lurks nearby. Smaller local museums often arrange exhibitions about the war, encouraging people to turn out their cupboards for wartime souvenirs.

Along the south and east coasts, reminders of the war still stand: huge concrete blocks, or 'tank traps', and concrete 'pill-boxes' from which the Home Guard could have shot invading soldiers. War memorials in church yards sometimes have a cluster of names under the words 'killed by enemy action', bringing home the horror of air raids and exploding bombs.

Every year brings something new to explain or illustrate the war. Personal reminiscences are published; new films are made; unexploded bombs are ploughed or fished up; and the wreckage of a plane, shot down in the Battle of Britain, suddenly comes to light in the depths of a dense wood.

Books about the war

Hundreds of books have been written about the war. I have found the ones in this list useful, and often funny. Some may be out of print and hard to find but it is worth asking the library to get them for you, if they can. The more difficult books are at the end of the list.

Growing up in World War Two by Kathleen Monham, Wayland Publishers Ltd., 1979.

One Child's War by Victoria Massey, Ariel Books (BBC), 1978.

How We Used to Live, 1936–1953 by Freda Kelsall, Macdonald & Co., 1981.

Pete and the Doodlebug, and other stories by Griselda Gifford, Macmillan Children's Books, 1983.

Goodnight Mister Tom by Michelle Magorian, Puffin, 1981.

Our Own Century by Islay Doncaster, Longman Focus on History series, 1971.

At the time of Winston Churchill by Paul Fincham, Longman Focus on History series, 1977.

Boy in the Blitz by Colin Perry, Leo Cooper, 1972.

The Real Dad's Army by Norman Longmate, Arrow Books, 1974.

Keep Smiling Through, The Home Front, 1939–45 by Susan Briggs, Weidenfeld & Nicolson, 1975.

Bombers and Mash, The Domestic Front 1939–45 by Raynes Minns, Virago, 1980.

Britain Under Fire: The Bombing of Britain's Cities 1940–45 by Charles Whiting, Century Hutchinson, 1986

Things to do in groups

1. Make a recording about the Dunkirk rescue attempt. One person could be a radio reporter who is interviewing some of the Dunkirk survivors, asking them about their escape. Someone else could interview a WVS helper. The interviews could then be linked to commentaries on the scene at the railway station where the men are being looked after.
2. In a group, discuss what a week during the London blitz must have been like. Then prepare an imaginary diary for this week. In the seven entries write about getting to work (chapter 7), queuing up for food (chapter 5), sleeping in a shelter (chapter 3) and so on.
3. Many older people still have wartime recipes tucked away in old cookery books or copies of the 'Food Facts' leaflet. Others still have their ration books. See if you can discover enough things of this kind to organise a 'wartime food' exhibition.
4. Make a recording of London on Victory night. Describe the crowds, the noise and the lighted streets. Include sound effects and interview some people in the 'crowd'.

Glossary

allies countries who help each other in war. Britain, the USA and Russia were allies; so were Germany, Italy and Japan

austerity strict, harsh or severe

blitz series of air raids by which the Germans hoped to break people's spirits and make them ready to surrender. Comes from German word *blitzkreig*, meaning 'lightning war'

to **camouflage** to disguise something by colouring or covering it

civil defence the work of defending the civilian population and providing medical services and Air Raid Precautions (ARP) wardens

to **detonate** to cause a bomb or mine to explode

dogfight a fight between aeroplanes in mid-air

economy something of a less good quality or standard than usual

emergency laws laws made at a time of national danger, giving the government powers to act quickly

evacuee someone who is *evacuated*, or sent away from dangerous areas, for safety

grenade small bomb or explosive shell, thrown by hand

identity card small card (blue for children, white for adults) with personal details, to prove who a person was

incendiary bomb small bombs dropped from aircraft to set fire to buildings where they fell

intelligence reports from secret agents

Luftwaffe the German air force

mobile canteen truck or van equipped as a canteen. It was driven where it was needed, to provide meals and hot drinks

ration-book small book of tickets or coupons which were given up when buying food, to make sure that everyone got a fair share. There were similar books of clothes coupons

refugees people seeking shelter from danger or trouble, after their homes are bombed or their country *invaded*

salvage waste materials, saved to help the war effort. Metal, paper and rubber were all collected as salvage

siren loud, high-pitched wailing noise, to warn of air raids. The up-and-down note told that a raid was beginning. The steady note was the 'all clear' or 'raiders passed' signal

stirrup pump small simple pump for fire-fighters. It worked from a bucket of water and had a long hose and nozzle